## LEADER'S GUIDE

THE
# SUPERNATURAL
# POWER
OF A
# TRANSFORMED
# MIND

# DESTINY IMAGE BOOKS BY BILL JOHNSON

# THE
# SUPERNATURAL
# POWER
## OF A
# TRANSFORMED
# MIND

## ACCESS TO A LIFE OF MIRACLES

# BILL JOHNSON

Leader's Guide prepared by Larry Sparks

DESTINY IMAGE® PUBLISHERS, INC.
P.O. Box 310, Shippensburg, PA 17257-0310
*"Promoting Inspired Lives."*

This book and all other Destiny Image, Revival Press, MercyPlace, Fresh Bread, Destiny Image Fiction, and Treasure House books are available at Christian bookstores and distributors worldwide.

For a U.S. bookstore nearest you, call 1-800-722-6774.
For more information on foreign distributors, call 717-532-3040.
Reach us on the Internet: www.destinyimage.com.

ISBN 13 TP: 978-0-7684-0456-2

For Worldwide Distribution, Printed in the U.S.A.
1 2 3 4 5 6 7 8 / 18 17 16 15 14

# CONTENTS

# CONTENTS

# BASIC LEADER GUIDELINES

This study is designed to help you develop into a believer who thinks from Heaven's perspective and walks out a lifestyle of power, authority, and faith. From *this* perspective, you will partner with God to see impossibilities bow at Jesus' name. And it all begins with a transformed mind!

There are several different ways that you can engage this study. By no means is this forthcoming list comprehensive. Rather, these are the standard outlets recommended to facilitate this curriculum. We encourage you to seek the Lord's direction, be creative, and prepare for supernatural transformation in your Christian life.

When all is said and done, this curriculum is unique in that the end goal is *not* information—it is transformation. The sessions are intentionally sequenced to take every believer on a journey from information, to revelation, to transformation. Participants will receive a greater understanding of what partnership with Heaven looks like and learn how to practically live this supernatural lifestyle on a daily basis.

Here are some of the ways you can use the curriculum:

## 1. CHURCH SMALL GROUP

Often, churches feature a variety of different small group opportunities per season, in terms of books, curriculum resources, and Bible studies. *The Supernatural Power of a Transformed Mind* would be included among the offering of titles for whatever season you are launching for the small group program.

It is recommended that you have at least four to five people to make up a small group, and a maximum of twelve. If you end up with more than twelve members, either the group needs to multiply and break into two different groups, or you should consider moving toward a church class model (which will be outlined next).

For a small group setting, here are the essentials:

*Meeting Place*
Either the leader's home, or a space provided by the church.

*Appropriate Technology*
A DVD player attached to a TV that is large enough for all of the group members to see (and loud enough for everyone to hear).

*Leader/Facilitator*
This person will often be the host, if the small group is being conducted at someone's home; but it can also be a team (husband/wife, two church leaders, etc.). The leader(s) will direct the session from beginning to end, from sending reminder e-mails to participating group members about the meetings, to closing out the sessions in prayer and dismissing everyone. That said, leaders might select certain people in the group to assist with various elements of the meeting: worship, prayer, ministry time, etc. A detailed description of what the group meetings should look like will follow in the pages to come.

*Sample Schedule for Home Group Meeting (for a 7:00 P.M. Meeting)*

- Before arrival: Ensure that refreshments are ready by 6:15 P.M. If they need to be refrigerated, ensure they are preserved appropriately until 15 minutes prior to the official meeting time.

- 6:15 P.M.: Leaders arrive at meeting home or facility.

- 6:15–6:25 P.M.: Connect with hosts, co-hosts, and/or co-leaders to review the evening's program.

- 6:25–6:35 P.M.: Pray with hosts, co-hosts, and/or co-leaders for the evening's events. Here are some sample prayer directives:

  - For the Holy Spirit to move and minister freely.
  - For the teaching to connect with and transform all who hear it.
  - For dialogue and conversation that edifies.
  - For comfort and transparency among group members.
  - For the Presence of God to manifest during worship.
  - For testimonies of answered prayers.
  - For increased hunger for God's Presence and power.

- 6:35–6:45 P.M.: Ensure technology is functioning properly!

- Test the DVDs featuring the teaching sessions, making sure they are set up to the appropriate session.

- If you are doing praise and worship, ensure that either the MP3 player or CD player is functional, set at an appropriate volume (not soft, but not incredibly loud), and that song sheets are available for everyone so they can sing along with the lyrics. (If you are tech savvy, you could do a PowerPoint or Keynote presentation featuring the lyrics.)

- 6:45–7:00 P.M.: Welcome and greeting for guests.

- 7:00–7:10 P.M.: Fellowship, community, and refreshments.

- 7:10–7:12 P.M.: Gather everyone together in the meeting place.

- 7:12–7:30 P.M.: Introductory prayer and worship.

- 7:30–7:40 P.M.: Ministry and prayer time.

- 7:40–8:00 P.M.: Watch DVD session.

- 8:00–8:20 P.M.: Discuss DVD session.

- 8:20–8:35 P.M.: Activation time.

- 8:35–8:40 P.M.: Closing prayer and dismiss.

This sample schedule is *not* intended to lock you into a formula. It is simply provided as a template to help you get started. Our hope is that you customize it according to the unique needs of your group, and sensitively navigate the activity of the Holy Spirit as He uses these sessions to supernaturally transform the lives of every person participating.

## 2. SMALL GROUP CHURCH-WIDE CAMPAIGN

This would be the decision of the pastor or senior leadership of the church. In this model, the entire church would go through *The Supernatural Power of a Transformed Mind* in both the main services and ancillary small groups/life classes.

These campaigns would be marketed as *40 Days of Transformation* or *40 Days of Transforming Your Mind*. The pastor's weekend sermon would be based on the principles in *The Supernatural Power of a Transformed Mind,* and the Sunday school classes/life classes and/or small groups would also follow the *Supernatural Power of a Transformed Mind* curriculum format.

## 3. CHURCH CLASS | MID-WEEK CLASS | SUNDAY SCHOOL CURRICULUM

Churches of all sizes offer a variety of classes purposed to develop members into more effective disciples of Jesus and agents of transformation in their spheres of influence.

*The Supernatural Power of a Transformed Mind* would be an invaluable addition to a church's class offering. Typically, churches offer a variety of topical classes, targeted at men's needs, women's needs, marriage, family, finances, and various areas of Bible study.

*The Supernatural Power of a Transformed Mind* is a unique resource, as it does not fit in with the aforementioned traditional topics usually offered to the Church body. On the contrary, this study breaks down a foundational truth of the Christian life—what it means to change the way you think—and takes it to a whole new level for all believers, showing them how to start living from Heaven's perspective, and supernaturally transform the world around them.

The benefit of *The Supernatural Power of the Transformed Mind* is that it builds on *whatever* foundation a believer may have already received about walking in the supernatural—whether the information they received was extremely basic, or they were taken further down the road and given some instruction on moving in signs and wonders.

While it may difficult to facilitate dialogue in a class setting, it is certainly possible and recommended. The other way to successfully engage *The Supernatural Power of the Transformed Mind* in a class setting is to have a teacher/leader go through the questions/answers presented in the upcoming pages and use these as his or her teaching notes.

## 4. INDIVIDUAL STUDY

While the curriculum is designed for use in a group setting, it also works as a tool that can equip anyone who is looking to strengthen his or her experience of partnering with God to transform their world.

# STEPS TO LAUNCHING A SUPERNATURAL POWER OF THE TRANSFORMED MIND GROUP OR CLASS

## PREPARE WITH PRAYER!

*Pray!* If you are a church leader, prayerfully consider how *The Supernatural Power of the Transformed Mind* could transform the culture and climate of your church community! The Lord is raising up bodies of believers that bring transformation in their wake because of the overflow of a mind that's been reoriented to Heaven's perspective. Spend some time with the Holy Spirit, asking Him to give you vision for what this unique study will do for your church, and, ultimately, how a Kingdom-minded people will transform your city and region.

If you are a group leader or class facilitator, pray for those who will be attending your group, signing up for your class, and will be positioning their lives to be transformed by the Power and Presence of God in this study.

## PREPARE PRACTICALLY!

*Determine* how you will be using *The Supernatural Power of a Transformed Mind* curriculum.

*Identify* which of the following formats you will be using the curriculum in:

- Church-sponsored small group study

- Church class (Wednesday night, Sunday morning, etc.)

- Church-wide campaign

- Individual study

*Determine a meeting location and ensure availability of appropriate equipment.*

Keep in mind the number of people who may attend. You will also need AV (audio-visual) equipment. The more comfortable the setting, the more people will enjoy being there and will spend more time ministering to each other!

A word of caution here: the larger the group, the greater the need for co-leaders or assistants. The ideal small group size is difficult to judge; however, once you get more than 10 to 12 people, it becomes difficult for each member to feel "heard." If your group is larger than 12 people, consider, either having two or more small group discussion leaders, or "multiplying" the larger group into two smaller ones.

*Determine the format for your meetings.*

The Presence of the Lord, which brings transformation, is cradled and stewarded well in the midst of organization. Structure should never replace spontaneity, but, on the contrary, having a plan and determining what type of format your meetings will take, enables you to flow with the Holy Spirit and minister more effectively.

Also, by determining what kind of meeting you will be hosting, you become well equipped to develop a schedule for the meeting, identify potential co-leaders, and order the appropriate quantity of resources.

*Set a schedule for your meetings.*

Once you have established the format for your meetings, set a schedule for your meetings. Some groups like to have a time of fellowship or socializing (either before or after the meeting begins), where light refreshments are offered. Some groups will want to incorporate times of worship and personal ministry into the small group or class. This is highly recommended for *The Supernatural Power of a Transformed Mind*, as the study is designed to be founded upon equipping and activating believers through encountering God's Presence. The video portion and discussion questions are intended to instruct believers, while the worship, times of ministry, group interaction, prayer time, and activation elements are purposed to engage them to live out what they just learned. *The Supernatural Power of the Transformed Mind* is not a lofty theological concept; it is a practical reality for every born-again believer. This study is intended to educate; but even more so, it is designed to activate believers and position them to steward the transformative power of a renewed mind.

*Establish a start date along with a weekly meeting day and time.*

This eight-week curriculum should be followed consistently and consecutively. Be mindful of the fact that while there are eight weeks of material, most groups will want to meet one last time after completing the last week to celebrate, or designate their first meeting as a time to get to know each other and "break the ice." This is very normal and should be encouraged to continue the community momentum that the small group experience initiates. Typically, after the final session is completed, groups will often engage in a social activity—either going out to dinner together, seeing a movie, or something of the like.

Look far enough ahead on the calendar to account for anything that might interfere. Choose a day that works well for the members of your group. For a church class, be sure to coordinate the time with the appropriate ministry leader.

### Advertise!

Getting the word out in multiple ways is most effective. Print out flyers, post a sign-up sheet, make an announcement in church services or group meetings, send out weekly e-mails and text messages, set up your own blog or website, or post the event on the social media avenue you and your group utilize most (Facebook, Twitter, etc…). A personal invitation or phone call is a great way to reach those who might need that little bit of extra encouragement to get involved.

For any type of small group or class to succeed, it must be endorsed by and encouraged from the leadership. For larger churches with multiple group/class offerings, it is wise to provide church members literature featuring all of the different small group/class options. This information should also be displayed online in an easily accessible page on your church website.

For smaller churches, it is a good idea for the pastor or a key leader to announce the launch of a small group course or class from the pulpit during an announcement time.

*Gather your materials.*

Group/Class Leaders, visit the website www.churchally.com to access special resources that will help you become comfortable with the material you will be presenting.

Each leader will need *The Supernatural Power of the Transformed Mind* Leader's Kit, as well as *The Supernatural Power of the Transformed Mind* book.

Additionally, each participant will need a personal copy of *The Supernatural Power of the Transformed Mind* study guide. It is recommended they also purchase *The Supernatural Power of the Transformed Mind* book for further enrichment, and as a resource to complement their daily readings. However, they *are* able to engage in the exercises and participate in the group discussion apart from reading the book.

We have found it best for the materials to all be purchased at one time—many booksellers and distributors offer discounts on multiple orders, and you are assured that each member will have their materials from the beginning of the course.

Visit www.churchally.com for special group discounts on ordering study guides and study materials, along with different package options.

## STEP FORWARD!

* Arrive at your meeting with plenty of time to prepare; frazzled, last-minute preparations do not put you in a place of "rest," and your group members will sense your stress! Ensure that all AV equipment is working properly and that you have ample supplies for each member.

Nametags are a great idea, at least for the first couple of meetings. Icebreaker and introduction activities are also a good idea for the first meeting.

- Pray for your members. As much as possible, make yourself available to them. As each person increases in insight on the transformed mind, they will want to share that discovery! You will also need to encourage those who struggle, grow weary, or lose heart along the journey and through the process. Make sure your members stay committed so they experience the full benefits of this teaching.

- Embrace the journey that you and your fellow members are embarking on to walk in the supernatural. Transformation begins within you!

- Multiply yourself. Is there someone you know who was not able to attend your group? Help them to initiate their own small group, now that you know how effective hosting The Supernatural Power of the Transformed Mind can be in a group setting!

### THANK YOU

Thank you for embarking on a journey that will sow into a modern renaissance in the church, and ultimately, position each participant to become an agent of supernatural transformation wherever God has placed you.

# LEADER CHECKLIST

*One to Two Months Prior*

_____ Have you determined a start date for your class or small group?

_____ Have you determined the format, meeting day and time, and weekly meeting schedule?

_____ Have you selected a meeting location (making sure you have adequate space and AV equipment available)?

_____ Have you advertised? Do you have a sign-up sheet to ensure you order enough materials?

*Three Weeks to One Month Prior*

_____ Have your ordered materials? You will need a copy of *The Supernatural Power of the Transformed Mind* leader's kit, along with copies of the study guide and book for each participant.

_____ Have you organized your meeting schedule/format?

*One to Two Weeks Prior*

_____ Have you received all your materials?

_____ Have you reviewed the DVDs and your Leader's Guide to familiarize yourself with the material, and to ensure everything is in order?

_____ Have you planned and organized your refreshments, if you are planning to provide them? Some leaders will handle this themselves, and some find it easier to allow participants to sign up to provide refreshments if they would like to do so.

_____ Have you advertised and promoted? This includes sending out e-mails to all participants, setting up a Facebook group, setting up a group through your church's database system (if available), promotion in the church bulletin, etc.

_____ Have you appointed co-leaders to assist you with the various portions of the group/class? While it is not necessary, it is helpful to have someone who is in charge of either leading (on guitar, keyboard, etc.) or arranging the worship music (putting songs on a CD, creating song lyric sheets, etc.). It is also helpful to have a prayer coordinator as well—someone who helps facilitate the prayer time, ensuring that all of the prayer needs are acknowledged and remembered, and assigning the various requests to group members who would be willing to lift up those needs in prayer.

### First Meeting Day

_____ Plan to arrive early! Give yourself extra time to set up the meeting space, double check all AV equipment, and organize your materials. It might be helpful to ask participants to arrive 15 minutes early for the first meeting to allow for distribution of materials and any icebreaker activity you might have planned.

# WEEKLY OVERVIEW OF MEETINGS/ GROUP SESSIONS

Here are some instructions on how to use each of the weekly Discussion Question guides.

### WELCOME AND FELLOWSHIP TIME (10-15 MINUTES)

This usually begins five to ten minutes prior to the designated meeting time and typically continues up until ten minutes after the official starting time. Community is important. One of the issues in many small group/class environments is the lack of connectivity among the people. People walk around inspired and resourced, but they remain disconnected from other believers. Foster an environment where community is developed but, at the same time, not distracting. Distraction tends to be a problem that plagues small group settings more than classes.

Welcome everyone as they walk in. If it is a small group environment, as the host or leader, be intentional about connecting with each person as they enter the meeting space. If it is a church class environment, it is still recommended that the leader connect with each participant. However, there will be less pressure for the participants to feel connected immediately in a traditional class setting, versus a more intimate, small group environment.

Refreshments and materials: In the small group, you can serve refreshments and facilitate fellowship between group members. In a class setting, talk with the attendees and ensure that they purchase all of their necessary materials (study guide and optional copy of *The Supernatural Power of the Transformed Mind*). Ideally, the small group members will have received all of their resources prior to Week 1, but if not, ensure that the materials are present at the meeting and available for group members to pick up or purchase. It is advisable that you have several copies of the study guide and book available at the small group meeting, just in case people did not receive their copies at the designated time.

Call the meeting to order. This involves gathering everyone together in the appropriate place and clearly announcing that the meeting is getting ready to start.

Pray! Open every session in prayer, specifically addressing the topic that you will be covering in the upcoming meeting time. Invite the Presence of the Holy Spirit to come, move among the group members, minister to them individually, reveal Jesus, and stir greater hunger in each participant to experience *more* of God's power in their lives.

## INTRODUCTIONS (10 MINUTES—FIRST CLASS ONLY)

While a time of formal introduction should only be done on the first week of the class/session, it is recommended that in subsequent meetings group members state their names when addressing a question, making a prayer request, giving a comment, etc., just to ensure everyone is familiar with names. You are also welcome to do a short icebreaker activity at this time.

(First Meeting) Introduce yourself, and allow each participant to briefly introduce him/herself. This should work fine for both small group and class environments. In a small group, you can go around the room and have each person introduce himself/herself one at a time. In a classroom setting, establish some type of flow and then have each person give a quick introduction (name, interesting factoid, etc.).

(First Meeting) Discuss the schedule for the meetings. Provide participants an overview of what the next eight weeks will look like. If you plan to do any type of "social activities," you might want to advertise this right up front, noting that while the curriculum runs for eight weeks, there will be a ninth session dedicated to fellowship and some type of fun activity.

(First Meeting) Distribute materials to each participant. Briefly orient the participants to the book and study guide, explaining the 15 to 20 minute time commitment for every day (Monday—Friday). Encourage each person to engage fully in this journey—they will get out of it only as much as they invest. The purpose for the daily reinforcement activities is *not* to add busywork to their lives. This is actually a way to cultivate a habit of Bible study and daily time renewing their minds, starting with just 15 to 20 minutes a day. Morning, evening, afternoon—*when* does not matter. The key is making the decision to engage.

## WORSHIP (15 MINUTES—OPTIONAL FOR THE FIRST MEETING)

Fifteen minutes is a solid time for a worship segment. That said, it all depends upon the culture of your group. If everyone is okay with doing 30 minutes of praise and worship, by all means, go for it!

For this particular curriculum, a worship segment is highly recommended, as true and lasting transformation happens as we encounter God's Presence.

If a group chooses to do a worship segment, usually they decide to begin on the second week. It often takes an introductory meeting for everyone to become acquainted with one another, and comfortable with their surroundings before they open up together in worship.

On the other hand, if the group members are already comfortable with one another and they are ready to launch immediately into a time of worship, they should definitely begin on the first meeting.

While it has been unusual for Sunday school/church classes to have a time of worship during their sessions, it is actually a powerful way to prepare participants to receive the truth being shared in *The Supernatural Power of a Transformed Mind* sessions. In addition, pre-service worship (if the class is being held prior to a Sunday morning worship experience), actually stirs hunger in the participants for greater encounters with God's Presence, both corporately and congregationally.

If the class is held mid-week (or on a day where there is *no* church service going on), a praise and worship component is a wonderful way to refresh believers in God's Presence as they are given the privilege of coming together, mid-week, and corporately experiencing Him.

## PRAYER/MINISTRY TIME (5-15 MINUTES)

At this point, you will transition from either welcome or worship into a time of prayer.

Just like praise and worship, it is recommended that this initial time of prayer be five to ten minutes in length; but if the group is made up of people who do not mind praying longer, it should not be discouraged. The key is stewarding everyone's time well, while maintaining focus on the most important things at hand.

There are real people carrying deep needs to the group and they need supernatural ministry. The prayer component is a time where group members will not just receive prayer, but also learn how to exercise Jesus' authority in their own lives, and witness breakthrough in their circumstances.

This prayer time doubles as a "ministry time," where believers are encouraged to flow in the gifts of the Holy Spirit. After the door is opened through worship, the atmosphere is typically charged with God's Presence. It is quite common for people to receive words of knowledge, words of wisdom, prophetic words, and for other manifestations of the Holy Spirit to take place (see 1 Cor. 12) in these times. This is a safe environment for people to "practice" these gifts, take risks, etc. However, if there are individuals who demonstrate consistent disorder, are unceasingly distracting, have problems/issues that move beyond the scope of this particular curriculum (and appear to need specialized counseling), or have issues that veer more into the theological realm, it is best for you to refer these individuals to an appropriate leader in the church who can address these particular items privately.

If you are such a leader, you can either point them to a different person, or you can encourage them to save their questions/comments and you will address them outside of the group context, as you do not want to distract from what God is doing in these vital moments together.

## Transition Time

At this point, you will transition from prayer/ministry time to watching *The Supernatural Power of the Transformed Mind* DVDs.

Group leaders/class teachers: It is recommended that you have the DVD in the player and are all ready to press "play" on the appropriate session.

## Video/Teaching (20-25 minutes)

During this time, group members will fill in the blanks in their participant study guides. All of the information they need to complete this assignment will appear on-screen, during the session. However, there will be additional information that appears on-screen that will not go in the "fill in the blank" section. This is simply for the viewer's own notation.

### DISCUSSION QUESTIONS (20-30 MINUTES)

In the *Leader's Guide*, each question will look like the following (see example below from Week 1):

- What does true repentance look like?
  - *Answer:* Repentance begins with godly sorrow over sin. However, it does not stay there. According to the Greek, repentance refers to a changing or transformation of the mind.

Some lessons will have more questions than others. Also, there might be some instances where you choose to cut out certain questions for the sake of time. This is entirely up to you, and in a circumstance where the Holy Spirit is moving and appears to be highlighting some questions more than others, flow in sync with the Holy Spirit. He will not steer you wrong!

First, you will have a question. Typically, it will lead with a Scripture verse (but not always). To engage group members, you can ask for volunteers to read the Scripture verse(s). As you ask the question in the group setting, encourage more than one person to provide an answer.

Second, we have provided a sample answer—which is one of the more concise responses in how to appropriately answer the question. This is a tool to help you navigate the conversation and ensure that everyone is on the same page when it comes to understanding the topic that the particular session covered. *Be sure to study and review the answer* so you are ready to confidently address questions, and field the answers provided by the group members.

Third, there is a very intentional flow in the order of questions. The questions will usually start out by addressing a problem, misconception, or false understanding, and are designed to take participants to a point of strategically addressing the problem, and then, take appropriate action.

The problem with many curriculum studies is in the question/answer section. Participants may feel like the conversation was lively, the dialogue insightful, and that the meeting was an overall success; but when all is said and done, the question, *"What do I do next?"* is not sufficiently answered.

This is why every discussion time will be followed with an activation segment.

### ACTIVATE (5-10 MINUTES)

- Each activation segment should be five to ten minutes at the minimum, as this is the place where believers start putting action to what they just learned.

- The activation segment will be tailored for the session covered.

- Even though every group member might not be able to participate in the activation exercise, it gives them a visual for what it looks like to demonstrate the concept that they just studied.

### TAKE AWAY

After the activation exercise, we have included a brief summary of the "Take Away" from that unique session. This is what participants should walk away from each session—knowing and applying.

### Plans for the Next Week (2 minutes)

Remind group members about daily exercises in the study guide. Encourage everyone to participate fully in this journey in order to get the most out of it. The daily exercises should not take more than 15 to 20 minutes and they will make an ideal 40-day themed Bible study.

Be sure to let group members know if the meeting location will change or differ from week to week, or if there are any other relevant announcements to your group/class. Weekly e-mails, Facebook updates, and text messages, are great tools to communicate with your group. If your church has a database tool that allows for communication between small group/class leaders and members, that is an effective avenue for interaction as well.

### Close in Prayer

This is a good opportunity to ask for a volunteer.

# HOW TO THINK FROM HEAVEN'S PERSPECTIVE

**Prayer Focus**: Ask the Lord to help every participant understand what it means to *repent*, not only dealing with sin, but stepping into a new way of thinking about reality.

## FELLOWSHIP, WELCOME, AND INTRODUCTIONS
### (20-30 MINUTES—FOR THE FIRST MEETING)

Welcome everyone as they walk in. If it is a small group environment, as the host or leader be intentional about connecting with each person as they come to the meeting space. If it is a church class environment, it is still recommended that the leader connects with each participant. However, there will be less pressure for the participants to feel connected immediately in a traditional class setting, versus a more intimate, small group environment.

In the small group, serve refreshments and facilitate fellowship between group members. In a class setting, talk with the attendees and ensure that they receive all of their necessary materials (the study guide and a copy of *The Supernatural Power of the Transformed Mind*).

Introduce yourself, and allow participants to briefly introduce themselves as well. This should work fine for both small group and class environments. In a small group, you can go around the room and have each person introduce him or herself, one at a time. In a classroom setting, establish some type of flow and then have each person give a quick introduction (name, interesting factoid, etc.).

Discuss the schedule for the meetings. Provide participants an overview of what the next eight weeks will look like. If you plan to do any type of "social activities," you might want to advertise this at the start, noting that while the curriculum runs for eight weeks, there will be a ninth meeting dedicated to fellowship and some type of fun activity. However, you might come up with this idea later on in the actual study.

Distribute materials to each participant. Briefly orient the participants to the book and study guide, explaining the 15 to 20 minute time commitment for each day. Encourage each person to engage fully in this journey—they will get out of it only as much as they invest. The purpose for the daily reinforcement activities is *not* to add busywork to their lives. This is actually a way to cultivate a habit of Bible study and daily time pursuing God's Presence, starting with just 15 to 20 minutes. Morning, evening, afternoon—*when* does not matter. The key is making the decision to engage.

## OPENING PRAYER

### WORSHIP (15 MINUTES—OPTIONAL FOR FIRST MEETING)

If a group chooses to do a worship segment, often they decide to begin on the second week. It usually takes an introductory meeting for everyone to become acquainted with one another and comfortable with their surroundings before they open up in worship.

On the other hand, if the group members are already comfortable with one another and they are ready to launch right into a time of worship, they should definitely go for it!

### PRAYER/MINISTRY TIME (5-15 MINUTES)

### VIDEO/TEACHING (20 MINUTES)

### DISCUSSION QUESTIONS (25-30 MINUTES)

* Read Romans 12:1-2. What does it mean that the renewed mind approves the will of God?

  * *Answer:* When our minds are renewed and are in agreement with Heaven's perspective, we will be able to clearly identify what is of God and what is not. The key is keeping our focus on Him.

* How does Bill's "Van Gogh" example help you understand what it means to approve God's will?

* What are some practical ways you can train your mind to clearly see who God is, what He is like, and what His will is? How have these methods helped train your mind to accurately see who God is and what His will is?

  * Get a few people to share their responses and how these methods have been effective for them.

  * Sample *Answers:* Reading Scripture, looking at the example of Jesus, the Gospels, internal witness of the Holy Spirit, etc.

- What are the two keys to thinking from Heaven's perspective? How do you apply these to everyday life?

  - *Answer:* 1) The renewed mind starts with how we think about God; 2) The renewed mind recognizes that God has a solution for every problem and He has made these solutions available to us.

- What does true repentance look like?

  - *Answer:* Repentance begins with godly sorrow over sin. However, it does not stay there. According to the Greek, repentance refers to a changing or transformation of the mind.

- How have you thought about repentance in the past?

  - Ask a few different group members and get their responses.

- How do the Gospels invite us to repent?

  - *Answers:* When we look at Jesus in the Gospels—His works, His words, and His thinking—our thinking is constantly challenged to "come up higher." Everything Jesus did calls us to transform how we think, especially when it comes to what we consider to be impossible.

### ACTIVATION: READ AND REPENT

With a new perspective on repentance, it is time to put our minds to work and truly *repent*.

- Invite the group to break up into smaller groups (of two to three).

- Assign them a chapter in the Gospels to read together (Mark is a great starting place). Specifically, identify a portion of Scripture where Jesus confronts an impossible situation (requiring a healing, deliverance, etc.). This should be the chapter everyone in the class/group focuses on.

- Challenge them to look at how Jesus responded to the impossibility and encourage them to discuss His perspective.

- At the end, have the group members pray for each other—specifically for the things in each other's lives that seem impossible.

## Take Away

The impossible becomes logical to the renewed mind. The gateway to experiencing transformation is repentance. Even though it begins with a godly sorrow over sin, repentance is designed to lead us into an altered approach to reality, where the model of Jesus sets the example for how we confront impossibility.

## Plans for the Next Week (2 minutes)

Point out Day 1 through Day 5 in the study guide. Encourage everyone to participate fully in this daily journey in order to get the most out of it.

## Close in Prayer

## Week 1

## VIDEO LISTENING GUIDE

1. Your beginning with Christ started with <u>repentance</u>.

2. Repentance: A godly sorrow over sin that produces a <u>shift</u> in how we think and see reality.

3. You know your mind is renewed when the <u>impossible</u> looks logical.

4. Faith does not come from the mind; it comes from the <u>heart</u>.

5. The renewed mind <u>enhances</u> faith.

6. Jesus' transfiguration is a <u>representation</u> of what the renewed mind looks like.

7. Thoughts <u>empower</u> the invisible—the unseen world.

8. There is a difference between what is in our <u>possession</u> and what is in our account.

*Keys to Thinking from Heaven's Perspective*

1. The renewed mind starts with how we think about <u>God</u>.

2. The renewed mind recognizes that God has <u>answers</u> to every problem and He has made these solutions available to us.

# YOUR MIND, GOD'S DWELLING PLACE

**Prayer Focus**: Ask the Lord to help every participant recognize his or her identity as a believer—they are the house of God. If the Presence of the Holy Spirit lives inside of them, every area of their lives should be impacted. To live like God's dwelling place, we need to begin thinking like God's house on the earth.

## FELLOWSHIP AND WELCOME (15-20 MINUTES)

Welcome everyone as they walk in. Be sure to identify any new members who were not at the previous session, have them introduce themselves so everyone is acquainted, and be sure that they receive the appropriate materials—study guide and book.

In the small group, serve refreshments and facilitate fellowship between group members. In a class setting, talk with the attendees—ask how their week has been and maintain a focus on what God *has done* and *is doing*.

Encourage everyone to gather in the meeting place. If it is a classroom setting, make an announcement that it is time to sit down and begin the session. If it is a small group, ensure everyone makes their way to the designated meeting space.

## OPENING PRAYER

## WORSHIP (15-20 MINUTES)

When it comes to the worship element, it can be executed in both small group and church class settings. While a worship time is not mandatory, it is highly encouraged, as the fundamental goal of this curriculum is to foster each participant's increased understanding and outworking of the supernatural realm. This is where true, lasting transformation takes place. Worship is a wonderful way of opening each session and setting everyone's perspective on what the study is about—not accumulating more information, but pursuing the One who is at the center of it all.

### PRAYER/MINISTRY TIME (5-15 MINUTES)

### VIDEO/TEACHING (20 MINUTES)

### DISCUSSION QUESTIONS (25-30 MINUTES)

- How can our minds limit God?

  - Get a few different responses.

  - *Answer:* Our minds limit God when we don't see Him as He truly is: unlimited in power and completely willing to move on our behalf. We also limit God when we believe lies about Him. Rather, we start believing false things about God and lies about who we are. Believing deception is what empowers the liar.

- After hearing Bill share about this reality that you are house of God—the house built on the edge of two worlds—why do you think it is so important to believe that this reality is true, that we are the dwelling place of God?

■ *Answer:* We become emboldened to carry God's power into different situations because we are confident of our identity. God Himself is with us; He is inside of us. When we start thinking from that perspective, nothing will be impossible to us, because it is no longer "us" by ourselves; we are indwelt by Almighty God!

- How does this truth change the way you think? (Specifically, about what you offer to those who are struggling, sick, tormented, bound and experiencing difficult circumstances?)

  ■ Get different answers.

- What does it mean that God "partners" with His people? Can you think of examples in Scripture where this has happened?

  ■ *Answer:* Even though God is completely sovereign and can act independently of us, He has chosen to partner together with us through collaboration to bring divine order to the planet.

- When you really believe that you are God's dwelling place, how does this change the way you pray for and minister to people?

  ■ *Answer:* When your first thought is "God lives inside of me," then you recognize that you actually carry His Presence and all that His Presence entails. In Romans 14:17, we see that the Kingdom of God is in the Holy Spirit. As you carry the Presence of the Holy Spirit, you bring the order, life, and divine solutions of the Kingdom of God into every situation in need of transformation. This is all because God lives inside of you and you have chosen to actually start believing this!

## ACTIVATION: PRAY LIKE YOU ARE GOD'S DWELLING PLACE

Based on what you just discovered about being God's dwelling place, it is time to put this reality into action.

- Break up into groups of two to three and pray for one another—specifically, personal needs (not needs of your family, friends, etc.—your specific needs). Share whatever you feel comfortable.

- The key is praying for each other directly, recognizing that we carry the Presence of God that releases the Kingdom of God.

- Pray with the understanding that God lives inside of you and He wants to bring divine order into your group members' situations.

- After praying for each other, evaluate. If you prayed for healing, ask the person if they feel any immediate improvement. Maybe you need to pray again! If it was more of an emotional or internal need, ask them to evaluate their condition. (How do they feel? What are they thinking?)

- If nothing happens immediately, do not be discouraged. Recognize the power of releasing God's Presence and power into the situation. You will have the ability to follow up next week and evaluate the level of improvement in those situations. (If possible, stay in touch with each other throughout the week.)

## TAKE AWAY

A key cornerstone of thought to moving in the supernatural is becoming convinced that God *really* does live inside of you.

## PLANS FOR THE NEXT WEEK (2 MINUTES)

Encourage group members to stay up to date with their daily exercises in the *Supernatural Power of a Transformed Mind study guide*.

## CLOSE IN PRAYER

## Week 2

## VIDEO LISTENING GUIDE

1. The more we discover how God thinks, the more it opens us up to <u>experience</u> Him differently.

2. We <u>restrict</u> what God is capable of doing in a situation because of our thought life.

3. The way we think either <u>cooperates</u> with God, or resists Him.

4. If we entertain thoughts in our minds that God does not entertain, we are entertaining a <u>lie</u>.

5. When we believe a lie, we <u>empower</u> the liar.

6. The house of God is built on the edge of two <u>worlds</u>.

7. Jesus was the initial <u>fulfillment</u> of the prophetic picture in Genesis 28.

8. The renewed mind enables us to live from God's <u>world</u> toward our world.

9. Whenever we speak God's words, we change people's <u>options</u>.

10. God can act independently of us, but He has chosen to <u>partner</u> with us.

11. Faith is to <u>explore</u> what revelation reveals.

# KEYS TO GROWING IN REVELATION

**Prayer Focus**: Ask the Lord to help the participants grow in their revelation and understanding of His thoughts.

### FELLOWSHIP AND WELCOME (10-15 MINUTES)

Welcome everyone as they walk in. Be sure to identify any new members who were not at the previous session, and be sure that they receive the appropriate materials—study guide and book.

### OPENING PRAYER

### WORSHIP (15-20 MINUTES)

### PRAYER/MINISTRY TIME (5-15 MINUTES)

### VIDEO/TEACHING (20 MINUTES)

### DISCUSSION QUESTIONS (25-30 MINUTES)

* Remember Peter's dialogue with Jesus in Matthew 16:22-23 (where Peter rebuked Jesus and then Jesus rebuked satan!). How is it possible to think from God's perspective in one moment and then think from the enemy's perspective in the next?

    * Get some different answers.

- *Answer:* It's all about what thoughts we decide to entertain. This is why it is so important to be constantly mindful of the ways of God. Otherwise, it is easy for us to quickly drift into carnal and even demonic thought patterns.

- What are some roadblocks to revelation?

  - *Answer:* 1) Humanity without Christ in the center and 2) personal ambition.

- How are these roadblocks dangerous to our thought lives?

  - Ask for different answers.

  - Answer 1: Humanity without Christ in the center places all of the emphasis on man, and man quickly becomes godlike.

  - Answer 2: Ambition is not evil in and of itself; however, if it is not checked in God's Presence and not Christ-centered in nature, our ambition can become carnal and self-focused very quickly.

- Let's discuss the three keys Bill lists to accessing revelation.

- What does childlikeness mean to you, and how is it important to receiving more revelation from God?

  - Ask for different answers.

  - *Answer:* Childlikeness keeps us in a position of humility and dependency before God. It constantly acknowledges that "we don't know it all," and as a result, invites more revelation!

- How does our willingness to obey attract revelation? Can you give an example of where your obedience to God brought greater clarity and revelation?

  - *Answer:* Saying "Yes" to God, even when we don't fully understand what He is asking us to do, reveals maturity. It is maturity that positions us to receive more, because increase is reserved for those who will steward what they already have well.

- What does it look like to be on the same "frequency as God"? How do you think biblical meditation (filling our minds with God's Truth) enables us to live on the same frequency as God, opening our ears to hear His voice and grow in revelation?

  - Ask for some different answers.

  - *Answer:* We need to fill our minds with God's thoughts. This is the first step to living on the same frequency as God. We can be Christians, but not think God's thoughts. One of the first decisions we need to make is to give our lives to biblical meditation.

### Activation: Biblical Meditation

Biblical meditation gets us on the same frequency as God.

- Encourage everyone to find their own place in the room where they can be alone with God.

- Here is their assignment: Find a passage in Scripture (a few verses at most) and for the next 10 minutes, meditate on it. Ponder it. Pray it. Write/journal about it.

- The key is learning how to embrace God's thoughts. Every verse in Scripture that shows us what God is like and reveals His nature is one of God's thoughts. In order to think like God, we need to discover how God thinks. Scripture is the primary vehicle that shows us who God is and what He thinks like.

- Ask a few people to share what their passage of Scripture revealed about how God thinks. This is how we should think.

### TAKE AWAY

We increase in revelation as we are willing to humble ourselves like children, say "Yes" to God through obedience, and get on Heaven's frequency through biblical meditation.

### PLANS FOR THE NEXT WEEK (2 MINUTES)

Encourage group members to stay up to date with their daily exercises in the *Supernatural Power of a Transformed Mind study guide*.

### CLOSE IN PRAYER

## Week 3

## VIDEO LISTENING GUIDE

*Roadblocks to Revelation*

1. Humanity without Christ in the center is <u>demonic</u> in nature.

2. <u>Ambition</u> can take you into the mind of man without you even knowing it.

*What Is True Meditation?*

1. Biblical meditation is to <u>ponder</u> something over and over again.

2. Biblical meditation is the <u>atmosphere</u> in which revelation thrives.

*Keys to Accessing Revelation*

1. Childlikeness <u>attracts</u> revelation.

   ▪ Every move of God starts with the <u>poor</u> in spirit.

   ▪ The drive to be <u>profound</u> ruins one's ability to hear from God.

2. The willingness to <u>obey</u> attracts revelation.

3. We must be on the same <u>frequency</u> as God in order to hear what He is saying.

# BECOME A STUDENT OF THE MIRACULOUS

**Prayer Focus:** Ask the Holy Spirit to give each participant clear understanding, as the following session is absolutely key in making the supernatural *sustainable* in their everyday lives.

## FELLOWSHIP AND WELCOME (10-15 MINUTES)

## OPENING PRAYER

## WORSHIP (15-20 MINUTES)

## PRAYER/MINISTRY TIME (5-15 MINUTES)

## VIDEO/TEACHING (25 MINUTES)

## DISCUSSION QUESTIONS (25-30 MINUTES)

- In the account of Jesus sleeping in the bottom of the boat during the storm—why do you think He rebuked the disciples?

  - Ask for different responses.

  - *Answer:* He rebuked them—even though they came down to ask Him to do something about the storm—because they did not receive an "education" from the past miracles they had seen Jesus perform.

- What do many people think the end result of a miracle is? What do you think Jesus wants the end result of a miracle to be?

  - Ask for different responses.

  - *Answer:* Many people think the end result of a miracle is receiving something from God, experiencing a personal breakthrough, or having something that was in a state of disorder made whole again. This is one dimension of the miraculous. The renewed mind is not content experiencing sporadic miracles, in the same way that Jesus was inviting His disciples into a lifestyle. Miracles are designed to teach us how to operate in the supernatural as a normal lifestyle. They also give visible expression to God's nature and character, showing us what He is like.

- How should miracles change the way you think?

  - *Answers:* They remind us of what Heaven looks like and constantly call us to represent God's world here on earth.

- What do you think Jesus wanted the disciples to learn from the loaves (that they should have applied in the storm situation)?

  - *Answer:* He wanted them to change the way they thought. They did not live from a world that experienced lack; they lived from a Kingdom that was full of abundance. In the same way, the world where Jesus lived had no storms. They were likewise called to represent this world on earth.

- Also, Jesus was inviting them to respond to the storm themselves, rather than come and ask Him about it. In the same way a word from Jesus was all the disciples needed to take food, divide it up, and see it supernaturally multiply in their hands, the word from Jesus telling them they were going to cross over to the other side of the sea should have been enough.

- Ask someone to share his/her testimony of how a miracle they experienced redefined how they saw God.

  - Note: Ask the Holy Spirit to lead you in this process. You might want to share a few more testimonies on this topic and then transition right into the activation segment after this.

### ACTIVATION: EDUCATED BY THE MIRACULOUS

Have the group/class break up into smaller groups of two to three people.

- Assignment: Have each participant share testimony of a miracle that God performed in his/her life (or a miracle they personally experienced that happened to someone else). The miracle is the teacher, and you are the students!

- Discuss: In the small groups, discuss with each other what that miracle says about: 1) who God is and 2) what God thinks about the situation your miracle turned around.

- Write down a brief description of the miracles you talk about, and next to the miracle, write the lesson that the miracle teaches about God.

- Pray: Declare the revelation of your past breakthrough over present circumstances. Whatever you discovered about God through the miracles you discussed, take that revelation and pray it over any situations that your fellow group members are presently going through. This should arm you with a new boldness in prayer. Remember, miracles reveal God's nature and God's thoughts.

## Take Away

Miracles alter the way we approach the circumstances and impossibilities we face in life. They reveal how God thinks and call us to adjust our thoughts to come into agreement with His.

## Plans for the Next Week (2 minutes)

Encourage group members to stay up to date with their daily exercises in *The Supernatural Power of the Transformed Mind study guide.*

## Close in Prayer

## Week 4

### VIDEO LISTENING GUIDE

1. Jesus' <u>word</u> enabled the food to multiply at the disciples' hands.

2. The same <u>decree</u> that multiplied food would also bring the disciples over to the other side of the sea.

3. Exposure to the miraculous challenges us to think <u>differently</u>.

*Three Leavens of the Mind*

1. Leaven of Herod—<u>Political</u> and humanistic in nature.

2. Leaven of the Pharisees—Religious mindset, where God is at the center, but He is impersonal and <u>powerless</u>.

3. Leaven of the <u>Kingdom</u> of God.
   - True faith is <u>superior</u> to all reasoning.
   - The leaven of Herod and the Pharisees are both driven by the <u>fear</u> of man.
   - When we can't see or hear what God is doing presently, we <u>remember</u> what He did last.

# HOW TO BELIEVE IN YOUR OWN SALVATION

**Prayer Focus**: Ask the Lord to bring freedom to every single participant, inviting the Holy Spirit to ground them in the eternal riches of what they received at salvation.

**FELLOWSHIP AND WELCOME** (10-15 MINUTES)

**OPENING PRAYER**

**WORSHIP** (15-20 MINUTES)

**PRAYER/MINISTRY TIME** (5-15 MINUTES)

**VIDEO/TEACHING** (20 MINUTES)

**DISCUSSION QUESTIONS** (25-30 MINUTES)

- Why do you think so many Christians have a tough time believing they are really, completely saved?

  - Ask for different answers.

- What happens when you are constantly questioning your salvation and your mind is never fully settled that you are holy, clean, and righteous in God's sight?

  - *Answer:* It short circuits us from living an effective, powerful Christian life. Our salvation is settled. The problem is not on God's end, but rather, what we think about our salvation. When we allow doubt to constantly enter our minds about our status before God, we will always feel unworthy and ultimately, unqualified to live a supernatural life.

- Why is identity such a key issue when it comes to living out a supernatural Christian life?

    - *Answer:* Confidence enables us to boldly fulfill our calling. If we truly believe that we are saved and called by God, we are confident that we can do what He said we can do.

- Can you list examples of people whom God called to do great things for Him, in spite of their shortcomings and failures?

    - *Answer:* Ask for difference responses.

- What is the significance of Sarah's story and how she is remembered in the book of Hebrews? How does this encourage you?

    - *Answer:* Even though Sarah made mistakes, when God wrote her story, it was defined by her faith, not her failures.

- Discuss the eight keys to fully believing in your salvation. Which key spoke to you the most?

    - Encourage as much group participation as possible, inviting each participant to share one of the keys that spoke to them most. (And, if they feel comfortable, ask them to share how that specific key helps them deal with a lie they have believed about salvation.)

## ACTIVATION: YOUR STORY FROM GOD'S POINT OF VIEW

- Ask everyone to get before the Lord. This may involve everyone finding a different place in the room to sit.

- Be sure they have some kind of writing device (electronic or paper).

- Have them ask the Father to share His version of their story. (In other words, how does God now see them because of the finished work of Jesus Christ?)

- It is very important that they write these observations down somewhere accessible—maybe on a phone or tablet.

- This can last from 10 to 15 minutes.

- At the end, ask one or two people if they are willing to share what the Holy Spirit told them.

## TAKE AWAY

Jesus' blood was entirely sufficient to save you from your sins and supernaturally transform your identity. He not only removed sin, but exchange your sin nature with His nature. Even though you still sin, you have lost the ability to enjoy it because of who is dwelling inside of you—the Holy Spirit.

## PLANS FOR THE NEXT WEEK (2 MINUTES)

Encourage group members to stay up to date with their daily exercises in *The Supernatural Power of a Transformed Mind study guide*.

## CLOSE IN PRAYER

## Week 5

## VIDEO LISTENING GUIDE

*8 Keys to Fully Believing in Your Salvation*

1. At salvation, you didn't lose the ability to sin; you lost the ability to <u>enjoy</u> sin.

2. As you are in Christ, the Father looks at you like He looks at <u>Jesus</u>.

3. When God records your story in His account, He only records what took place after <u>repentance</u>.

4. To revisit the past apart from the blood of Jesus is to open oneself up to a spirit of <u>deception</u>.

5. Your past can separate you from your <u>awareness</u> of the love of God.

6. God both forgives sin and removes the <u>nature</u> from which sin came.

7. When we see people as forgiven and as saints, we treat them <u>differently</u>.

8. The enemy frequently addresses the lie of <u>identity</u>.

*Keys to Being Anchored in Your Identity*

1. We <u>settle</u> into what God has said.

2. Get identity from <u>who</u> called us.

# THE POWER OF REMEMBERING

**Prayer Focus**: Ask the Lord to build a culture of testimony among the participants where His works, miracles, and acts start to become normal conversation.

### FELLOWSHIP AND WELCOME (10-15 MINUTES)

### OPENING PRAYER

### WORSHIP (15-20 MINUTES)

### PRAYER/MINISTRY TIME (5-15 MINUTES)

### VIDEO/TEACHING (20 MINUTES)

### DISCUSSION QUESTIONS (25-30 MINUTES)

- When you hear the word testimony, what do you immediately think of?

  - Get different responses.

- Based on Revelation 19:10 and what Bill shares in this session, how do you understand the concept of testimony in a different way?

  - *Answer:* Testimony is a record of anything that Jesus does, from saving us to healing us to delivering us. It is a record of His mighty acts.

- What are some practical ways that you can constantly focus on testimony?

  - Get different responses.

- Why do you think it is so important to constantly be talking about what God is doing? How does sharing testimony impact our thinking?

  - *Answer:* It is important to share testimony because as you remain vitally connected to stories of what God is doing and how He is moving, your faith remains stirred. Sharing testimony protects us from small thinking.

- Read Psalm 78:41. How does testimony protect you from thinking small and limiting God? And how is it possible to actually limit God?

  - *Answer:* By keeping ourselves continuously exposed to accounts of God's power and miracles, we are reminded that there are no impossibilities or restrictions for the God we serve. He is unlimited. We cannot limit Him, but we limit what we experience of Him because of how we think about Him.

- What do you think happens when people share testimony? How does your testimony have the ability to stir up faith in those listening to you?

  - *Answer:* Your testimony prophesies over the people who are listening, reminding them that the God who moved supernaturally for you can also move for them.

<h2 align="center">ACTIVATE: TESTIFY AND PRAY!</h2>

Feel free to limit the discussion time to focus on the Activation Exercise.

- Ask every group member to participate, if they feel comfortable.

- Go around the room, and ask each person to share testimony of something that God has done in his/her life.

  - Examples: healing, saving a family member, breaking addiction, restoring relationships—it can be anything. (Remind them to share the testimony honestly, not to exaggerate or downplay it; just be real and authentic!)

- For example, if the person shares testimony about how God supernaturally saved a lost loved one, they can ask the group, "How many people have lost family members you want to see come to Jesus?" Those with this particular need would raise their hands, and the person who just shared the faith-stirring testimony will proceed to release the power of the testimony over these needs through prayer.

- It would be a good idea to follow up next week and ask people to share testimonies of how this activation exercise released any measure of breakthrough in their situations.

## Take Away

Remembering what God has done keeps us vitally connected to His reality, His power, and His ability to perform the miraculous. As you remain conscious of the God who invades the impossible, your thinking expands and you begin to see circumstances differently.

## Plans for the Next Week (2 minutes)

Encourage group members to stay up to date with their daily exercises in *The Supernatural Power of the Transformed Mind study guide.*

## Close in Prayer

## Week 6

## VIDEO LISTENING GUIDE

1. When the supernatural invasions of God become removed from our <u>conversation</u>, we expect them even less.

2. Supernatural interaction with God maintains our <u>courage</u> to obey during difficulty and impossibility.

3. If you do not walk in a lifestyle of radical obedience, you become <u>cowardly</u> in conflict.

4. When you lose awareness of the God who invades the impossible, you will start thinking too <u>small</u>.

5. When we stop living conscious of the God who invades the impossible, we begin to reduce <u>ministry</u> to our gifts.

6. Be <u>accurate</u> when you share testimony.

*Benefits of Testimony*

1. The <u>culture</u> of testimony creates an environment where the invasions of God are continuous and ongoing.

2. If you remain conscious of what God has done in the past, it will empower you to be <u>confident</u> in a present circumstance.

# ENDURING UNCERTAINTY

**Prayer Focus**: Ask the Lord to help keep every participant grounded in what is sure and what is true about who He is—especially in seasons of difficulty and challenge.

## FELLOWSHIP AND WELCOME (10-15 MINUTES)

## OPENING PRAYER

## WORSHIP (15-20 MINUTES)

Feel free to shorten the worship time at the beginning of the session, as the activation exercise will consist of a worship segment.

## PRAYER/MINISTRY TIME (5-15 MINUTES)

## VIDEO/TEACHING (20 MINUTES)

## DISCUSSION QUESTIONS (25-30 MINUTES)

* What does it mean to "reduce the will of God to what is seen?"

  ▪ Get different answers.

  ▪ *Answer:* This is a popular approach to how people view God's will. Simply put, they believe that anything that happens in life is the direct responsibility of God. His will engineered and orchestrated it, both good and bad. There is no concept of a struggle, where you have an enemy who also has a will.

- Why do you think it is dangerous to label everything that happens in life as God's perfect will?

  - *Answer:* We start blaming God for things He is not responsible for. As a result, we begin to see Him differently.

- What lesson about disappointment did you learn from John the Baptist (based on Matthew 11)?

  - *Answer:* That it is easy to lose focus on what God is doing, especially when you are experiencing challenging circumstances. John the Baptist was in prison, and the One who came to "set captives free" did not come to rescue him.

- How does focusing on what God has done and is doing keep you encouraged?

  - *Answer:* Testimony protects us from falling into the ditch of disappointment and discouragement.

- Why do you think discouragement and disappointment are so dangerous to believers?

  - *Answer:* It causes us to start redefining who God is. Instead of believing that He is who Scripture reveals Him to be, we start basing our concept of God on what we perceive did not happen. Discouragement paints a new theology of who God is, and as a result, we do not see Him accurately.

- Discuss the keys to navigating through disappointment. (See if there is anyone willing to share a story of how they got through a disappointment.)

  - *Answer:* 1) Keep promises before us constantly; 2) celebrate God's goodness through praise.

- How does Bill's story about his dad passing away impact the way you view praise—specifically, offering praise in the midst of uncertainty?

  - Get different answers.

## ACTIVATE: CELEBRATE GOD'S GOODNESS THROUGH PRAISE

- Ask each person to think about a current need they have in prayer—particularly something that seems impossible.

- Either using audio tracks or a live worship leader, take this time to celebrate God's goodness—even in the midst of uncertainty.

- Instead of praying over the requests, invite each person to consider who God is in relation to their unique prayer request. Encourage them to praise God for who He is.

- The key is becoming focused on who He is and what He is doing. It is not about pretending away the problem; rather, it is seeing the problem in proportion to God.

## TAKE AWAY

During times of uncertainty, confusion, and discouragement, it is vital to focus on who God is and what He is doing. If we do not, we run the risk of altering the way we think about and respond to God based on our circumstances, rather than viewing Him based on what unchanging truth reveals.

## PLANS FOR THE NEXT WEEK (2 MINUTES)

Encourage group members to stay up to date with their daily exercises in *The Supernatural Power of the Transformed Mind study guide.*

## CLOSE IN PRAYER

## Week 7

## VIDEO LISTENING GUIDE

1. We cannot reduce the will of God to what we have <u>seen</u> happen.

2. If you feed yourself on what God has done, and is doing, you can always stay <u>encouraged</u>.

3. <u>Offense</u> with God leads to unbelief and resistance to the purposes of God.

4. We cannot afford to think about our present or future <u>differently</u> than God does.

*Keys to Navigating Through Disappointment*

1. Keep <u>promises</u> before us constantly.

2. <u>Celebrate</u> God's goodness through praise.

# DREAMING WITH GOD

**Prayer Focus**: Ask the Lord to give everyone a renewed vision of their friendship with God. It is out of this place of intimacy that they are free to boldly dream, desire, and create.

## FELLOWSHIP AND WELCOME (10-15 MINUTES)

## OPENING PRAYER

## WORSHIP (15-20 MINUTES)

## PRAYER/MINISTRY TIME (10 MINUTES)

## VIDEO/TEACHING (20 MINUTES)

## DISCUSSION QUESTIONS (25-30 MINUTES)

- Read Psalm 37:4. How have you thought about this verse in the past?

  - Ask for different answers.

- How does it make you feel to know that God actually wants you to have dreams and desires (that He actually makes Himself vulnerable to the desires of His people)?

  - Ask for different answers.

- What does the following statement mean to you: "God disciplines us because He wants our will to be done"? What do you think Bill means when he says this?

  - *Answer:* God does not make robots. He created us with free will and also, He has invited us into a place of friendship, intimacy, and collaboration. In the end, we reflect God most when—as free-thinking, choosing, and desiring people—we pursue dreams that carry and reveal His nature.

- Why do you think many believers are so nervous about pursuing their dreams? List some reasons that have held you back from pursuing certain dreams and desires.

  - Get different answers.

  - *Answer:* Many believers are afraid that their desires are not "in sync" with God's will.

- Based on what you read in Scripture (John 14:13-14, John 15:7, John 16:23), what is Jesus saying to His people about what they are able to desire and dream?

  - *Answer:* We can ask whatever we desire and He will do it for us.

- How can we know if our desires reflect God's heart and nature?

  - *Answer:* We bring them to God in His Presence. In fact, pay attention to dreams or desires that come up while you are in God's Presence, not just seeking

Him for a dream, but enjoying your relationship
with Him.

### ACTIVATE: DREAMING IN THE PRESENCE

- Have everyone get alone with the Lord (and again, have
  some type of writing instrument).

- Encourage them to dream. No limits. No restrictions.
  Nothing too outlandish or extreme.

- Invite each person to write down as many dreams as
  they can think of. (Take 10 to 15 minutes to do this.)

- Then, have everyone spend 10 minutes in God's
  Presence. Ask them to pay attention to what the Holy
  Spirit highlights on their "dream lists."

- This is not designed to be a "one time" event.
  Encourage participants to make this a regular habit,
  coming into God's Presence and evaluating what
  dreams/desires are highlighted in that place of intimacy.

### TAKE AWAY

One of the powerful end results of the transformed mind is a
people who dream with God. They do not place limitations or
restrictions on these dreams, as there are no limitations on the
God they have been invited to dream with.

## Plans for the Next Week (2 minutes)

Let participants know that either this is the final week of the study or that you will be having some type of social activity on the following week—or at a specified future date.

## Close in Prayer

Pray that the group would experience true transformation and power in their lives as they continue to daily walk using the tools that have been given throughout the study.

## Week 8

## VIDEO LISTENING GUIDE

1. God makes Himself <u>vulnerable</u> to the desires of His people.

2. The Lord wants to unveil His purposes in the earth through the dreams and desires of His <u>people</u>.

3. Often we crucify the <u>resurrected</u> man in the name of discipleship.

4. The inside of the Kingdom is <u>bigger</u> than the outside.

5. Creativity is needed in the place of <u>influence</u>.

6. God will always say "no" to whatever <u>undermines</u> our purpose.

7. Much of the church is waiting for the next command from the Lord; He is waiting to hear the <u>dreams</u> of His people.

8. Pay attention to the desires that come up as you are in God's <u>Presence</u>.

# LOOKING FOR MORE FROM BILL JOHNSON AND BETHEL CHURCH?

*Purchase* additional resources—CDs, DVDs, digital downloads, music—from Bill Johnson and the Bethel team at the online Bethel store.

Visit www.bjm.org for more information on Bill Johnson, to view his speaking itinerary, or to look into additional teaching resources.

To order Bethel Church resources, visit http://store.ibethel.org.

*Subscribe* to Bethel.TV to access the latest sermons, worship sets, and conferences from Bethel Church.

To subscribe, visit www.bethel.tv.

*Become* part of a Supernatural Culture that is transforming the world and *apply* for the Bethel School of Supernatural Ministry.

For more information, visit www.ibethel.org/school-of-ministry.